Explore The Emo
With Mel & Pip
&
The Magic Snow Globe

A collection of fun and thought-provoking short stories for children. This second book in the Mel & Pip series focuses on managing negative emotions and enjoying more positive ones.

Author: Beverley Davies

Illustrator: Nhi Nguyen

ISBN 9798837133992

CONTENTS

Welcome Back to My Magical World   1

Can We Really Feel Like Butterfly
Calm?   5

Has Butterfly Happy Always Felt
So Good?   28

What Can We Do to Feel More Like
Butterfly Proud?   44

What Helps Butterfly Believe Be So
Kind?   58

Where Is Sadness Hiding?   86

How Can We Help Butterfly Anxious?   112

Who Is Butterfly Disgust Talking To?   137

Will Butterfly Anger Ever Learn?   158

Final Words from Mel & Pip   183

Welcome Back to My

Magical World with Pip!

Hello again lovely reader. Pip and I

are so very pleased you are reading

our second book. We are both very

excited to have you with us again!

In our latest adventures, Pip and I return to the beautiful butterfly farm we visited during our last adventure. Each day we go to visit, we spend time with one of the special butterflies again.

It is at the butterfly farm that we learn some really helpful things about how to enjoy better feelings from

Butterfly Believe, Butterfly Happy, Butterfly Calm, and Butterfly Proud.

We also find ways to help Butterfly Sadness, Butterfly Anxious, Butterfly Anger and Butterfly Disgust.

With the help of a little bit of magic, a very clever cat, and a very special snow globe of course!

Don't worry if you haven't read our first book. You'll soon get to know all about me, my clever cat Pip, and the magic snow globe.

So, let's start our adventures together and see the beautiful

butterflies that have emotions you

may experience yourself sometimes.

Can We Really Feel Like Butterfly Calm?

So, lovely reader, are you ready to visit the butterfly farm with us?

I'm really excited about going back because I enjoy learning new

things. I also really want to see the beautiful butterflies again. I want to spend more time with each of them, so that I can understand more about each emotion.

So, I ask Pip if we can go back and see Butterfly Calm first. I have noticed that when I feel calm, I make better decisions. I also react to things in a more helpful way.

So, who better to learn from than Butterfly Calm?

Pip nodded his head and jumped up onto my bed. Once

again, he pointed his tail at the snow globe. As the orange light came out of the end of his tail, my snow globe lit up like magic and glowed bright orange. Then Pip said:

'*Tickety-Dee, Tickety-Boo,*
What does Butterfly Calm really do?
Tickety-Boo, Tickety-Dee,
Let him show us – just wait and see.'

Oh, how exciting! We are back at the butterfly farm! It looked as beautiful as it did the last time we were here! Once again there were hundreds of butterflies in many different colours. They were red and yellow and pink and green, purple and orange and blue. All the colours of a rainbow!

We start to walk to Butterfly Calm's favourite place at the edge of the field. Yes, he is there! Just resting on the tree branch as he had been before.

As we walk towards him, I say, "Hello again Butterfly Calm, it's Mel and Pip. We've come to see you again. Do you remember us?"

"Well hello Mel, and hello Pip," he said. "Of course, I remember you! It is so lovely to see you both again."

I then asked Butterfly Calm if he could tell us how he stays so calm. It could help some of the other butterflies who struggle with their emotions. I also said we wanted to help our lovely readers and ourselves learn to be calm, just like him.

Especially when we start to feel really emotional about things.

Butterfly Calm told us he practises **Mindfulness** every day.

"What is **Mindfulness**?" I asked Butterfly Calm.

He said it was about being in the present moment – he called it the 'here and now.' He said the best way to practice this is by putting all our attention on the things around us. Or on what we are doing at the time. Just taking our time and slowly noticing. Without any rush at all.

Then he said. "There are two things I practice each day. First, I start with what I call **Balloon Breathing**.

BREATHE

I imagine a pink balloon inside my tummy. As I breathe in, I imagine the balloon getting bigger as it fills with calm pink air. When I breathe out, I imagine the balloon getting smaller. I do this three times.

Next, I play my **Mindful** game of **5-4-3-2-1.**

5 is for five things I can see

4 is for four things I can touch or feel

3 is for three things I can hear

2 is for two things I can smell

1 is for one thing I can taste

I'll show you how I practice both. Just watch and listen."

Then he took three long, slow deep breaths - in and out. When he finished, he started talking in a calm and slow voice.

"**5** - I can see the lovely blue sky above me. White fluffy clouds in the sky. Colourful butterflies flying around. The beautiful white flowers on this branch. Trees swaying in the breeze.

4 - I can feel the warm sunshine on my wings. The breeze as it passes me by. The branch I am resting on. The flowers as I reach out to them.

3 - I can hear the birds singing next to me. The bees buzzing around. The young butterflies playing and having fun.

2 - I can smell the scent of the

flowers. The lovely smell of lavender.

1 - I can taste the nectar from the flowers. It tastes so good!

   I do so love this feeling of calmness."

Then he looked at Pip.

"Now it's your turn to practice **Mindfulness**, Pip. You can practice **Mindfulness** here, or anywhere you choose."

Pip looked very thoughtful. He said he wanted to practice in our garden.

The next thing I could hear was

Pip saying:

'Tickety-Boo, Tickety-Dee,

It is in our garden I wish to be,

Tickety-Dee, Tickety-Boo,

Mindfulness is what I need to do.'

To my surprise, Pip, Butterfly
Calm, and I were all in the garden
together.

Pip laid on the grass and took three slow deep breaths - in and out.

Then in a calm voice, he said:

"**5** - I can see Mel's red tree swing. The yellow ball we were playing with earlier. The long grass at the back of the garden. Mel's open bedroom window. The squirrel running beside the fence.

4 - I can feel the sunshine warming my golden fur. The wind in my whiskers. The soft grass I am laying on. My muscles relax as I have a big stretch and yawn.

3 - I can hear grasshoppers playing in the hedge. Soft music coming from the kitchen window. I can hear myself purring louder as I enjoy laying in the warm sunshine.

2 - I can smell Mel's mum baking cakes. I can smell the sausages being cooked on next door's barbeque.

1 - I can imagine tasting those delicious sausages! My mouth is watering as I lick my lips at the thought of it!

I totally agree with you Butterfly Calm," said Pip when he finished. "This **5-4-3-2-1** game makes me feel so nice and relaxed that I could have cat nap!

Now it's your turn to practice **Mindfulness**, Mel. Where will you choose your place to be?"

My favourite place has always been the seaside, so I told Pip that is

where I would like to go.

Once again, Pip looked at the
snow globe and said:

'Tickety-Boo, Tickety-Dee,
The seaside it is for Mel to be,
Tickety-Dee, Tickety-Boo,
Mindfulness is what she needs to do.'

Just like magic, we were all at the seaside! How exciting!

As the other two had done before me, I took in a big deep breath. As I breathed in, I imagined breathing in the lovely calm pink colour into the balloon inside my tummy. As I breathed out, I could imagine the balloon getting smaller. I did this three times.

Now I was ready to play the **Mindfulness** game of **5-4-3-2-1**. In a calm voice, I said:

"**5** - I can see miles of blue sea that looks like it touches the sky. Sailing boats in the distance, with tall white sails. People running into the sea. A really cute dog digging in the sand. A small boy building a sandcastle.

4 - I can feel the soft sand in my toes as I walk along the beach. The cold water as I start to walk into the sea to get to the paddle boat that I want to sit in. The lovely warm sun on my skin. The gentle breeze, ever so slightly moving my hair.

3 - I can hear seagulls squawking as they fly around in the sky. Children laughing as they play games on the sand. The waves as they come towards the shore.

2 - I can smell the coconut suntan lotion on my warm skin. Chips being

cooked in the café behind me. This is making me feel hungry!

1 - And now for the best taste in the whole world! The delicious taste of ice cream. A '99' with a chocolate flake and lots of strawberry sauce. Yummy!"

When I finished, I felt so calm and peaceful. I had a lovely warm feeling in my tummy.

Yes, I'm definitely going to practice **Mindfulness** every day, wherever I am. Just like Butterfly Calm does.

Butterfly Calm then told us about another helpful game he plays called 'blowing bubbles.' I'll tell you all about that later in the book, when we talk to Butterfly Anger, as I think it might be helpful for her.

It was time for us to say goodbye to Butterfly Calm. He needed to return to the butterfly farm and we needed to go home.

So, lovely reader, where will you practice your **Mindfulness**?

It can be practised anywhere at all, indoors or outdoors.

Just remember:

First, use an imaginary balloon,

To help you feel calm very soon,

Butterfly Calm says we need to think,

Of breathing in the colour pink,

To help us let difficult feelings go,

We just breathe out, nice and slow,

Then pay attention to where you are,

You'll soon be a Mindfulness star!

5 is for the lovely things we can see,

4 is for the sounds all around me,

3 is for the things we can touch,

2 is for the smells we like so much,

1 is for that yummy taste,

Ooh, this is such a lovely place,

So, practice Mindfulness each day,

As it's such a helpful game to play.

Has Butterfly Happy Always Felt So Good?

Hello again lovely reader. Another day, and another emotion for us to explore. This means another clever butterfly to talk to! I am really looking forward to another visit to the butterfly farm, and I hope you are too!

This time I ask Pip if we can go back and see Butterfly Happy. I am wondering if he has always been so happy, and what he does to feel so happy. I want to know if there is a secret to his joy and happiness. I want to know what kind of things he does to stay happy.

I also want to share everything I learn with you, my lovely reader. So, who better to learn from than Butterfly Happy?

Once again, Pip nodded his head and jumped up onto my bed. Once again, he pointed his tail at the snow globe. Once again, the orange light came out of the end of his tail and my snow globe lit up like magic!

Then Pip said:

'Tickety-Dee, Tickety-Boo,
What does Butterfly Happiness do?
Tickety-Boo, Tickety-Dee,
Take us to him, to ask him and see.'

We soon arrived at the butterfly farm, and right in front of us was Butterfly Happy. He was talking to some other butterflies, but he paused when he noticed us.

He said, "Hello again, Mel and Pip. How lovely it is to see you both. I have been spending some time with these lovely friends of mine. Can I

help you with anything today?"

I asked Butterfly Happy if he could tell us how he stays so happy, so that we could help some of the other butterflies that would like to feel happier. I also said we would like to help our lovely readers and ourselves to learn to be happy like him.

Butterfly Happy said. "I haven't always felt so happy Mel. In fact, I have had times when I have felt really, really sad and lonely. I know it is normal to feel sad sometimes, but it feels so horrible to feel sad all of the

time. That is why I started to write down three very important things each day that help me to feel happy. Let me show you how this works for me. Hopefully it will work for you too."

I said, "If it works for you Butterfly Happy, then we would like to learn about what you do, wouldn't we Pip?"

Pip nodded his head in agreement.

"I call it my **1-2-3** game," said Butterfly Happy. "I write,

1 thing I like about myself

2 things I am good at

3 things I am grateful for

I write these things down each morning as I wake up. I also remind myself of them each night before I go to sleep. That way I get to focus on what really matters to me - all of the good things in my life."

I told Butterfly Happy and Pip that I really liked this idea and I really wanted to practice it myself.

We thanked Butterfly Happiness for his help and said

goodbye. He then flew off to play with his friends.

Then I heard Pip say:

'*Tickety-Dee, Tickety-Boo,*
Let's see if this can work for you,
Tickety-Boo, Tickety-Dee,
Let us play the game 1-2-3.'

We arrived back at the room we had been in before. The one with the large white screens on the wall. Only this time there were three screens. I looked at the first screen.

SOMETHING I LIKE ABOUT ME ....

There were the words **SOMETHING I LIKE ABOUT ME..........** written on it. Pip told me that I just needed to fill in the gap, and so I did. I thought about it and wrote:

I am kind to people

On the second screen, there were the words **I AM GOOD AT..........** written down twice.

Pip said I needed to write down two things this time.

I AM GOOD AT ....
I AM GOOD AT ....

So, I wrote:

I am good at spelling

I then tried to think of another

one. What else am I good at? Let me

think. Yes, I am good at running, and so I wrote that down.

I am good at running

Then I looked at the third board. The words **I AM GRATEFUL FOR** .... were written down three times.

Pip said that I needed to think about any three things I was grateful for. He said it could be things I have, things I can do, people in my life, or anything else I can think of.

So, I had a good think.

After a few minutes or so, I was

ready to write again. I wrote:

I AM GRATEFUL FOR............
I AM GRATEFUL FOR ....
I AM GRATEFUL FOR ....

I am grateful for my lovely cat Pip who helps me to learn lots of new things

I am grateful for my lovely bedroom and my comfy bed

I am grateful for my two best friends in the whole world

I do like this game a lot. So, what have I learnt with the help of a little magic?

When I play the game 1-2-3,

It makes me feel so very happy,

I write down 1 thing I like about me,

How hard can this really be?

I then write 2 things I am good at,

I can find 2, how good is that?

Then I write 3 things I am grateful for,

I feel more joyful than I did before,

All these things help me to see,

That it really is good to be me!

So, if you play the game 1-2-3,

You can feel like Butterfly Happy.

So, practice 1-2-3 each day,

As it's such a helpful game to play.

42

So, lovely reader, when will you practice your **1-2-3**?

Why not write it down in a special book like I do?

What Can We Do to Feel More Like Butterfly Proud?

Hello again, lovely reader. Yet another day and another emotion for us to understand. So, let's go back to the butterfly farm.

Today I ask Pip if we can go back and see Butterfly Proud. I am wondering what she does to feel so proud of herself.

The last time we saw her she was singing and feeling so good about herself and her life. I am curious to find out what she does. Are you, my lovely reader? Are you feeling curious today? Who better to learn from than Butterfly Proud?

Let's go and see her!

Pip jumped up onto my bed as usual. Once again, he pointed his tail at the snow globe. Once again, the orange light came out of the end of his tail and my snow globe lit up like magic!

Then Pip said:

'Tickety-Dee, Tickety-Boo,
What does Butterfly Proud really do?
Tickety-Boo, Tickety-Dee,
Let her show us – just wait and see.'

When we arrived at the butterfly farm, we could hear some lovely singing. It was coming from high up in the trees. We both looked up, and there she was! The beautiful orange coloured Butterfly Proud.

When she heard me and Pip talking below her, she called out to us.

"How lovely that you have come back to the beautiful butterfly farm. Mel and Pip, isn't it? How lovely to see you both again!

I have just been adding some little notes to my **Well-Done Jar**. It's hanging in the tree. Can you see it sparkling in the sunshine?"

I said, "That is the loveliest jar I have ever seen in my life, Butterfly Proud! It really does sparkle in the sunshine. I can see lots of notes inside. In lots of different colours too. Can

you tell me and Pip more about it

please, Butterfly Proud?"

She said, "Well of course I can. I will be very happy to show you. I had so much fun decorating my jar. Each day I get to fill it with nice words. I do think everyone should have one.

Let me explain to you what I do. If you can write these things down Mel, you will not forget them when you get back home."

"That is such a great idea, Butterfly Proud. But I don't have my book with me today."

"Here you are, Mel," said Pip as he gave me my book and pencil.

It was as if it appeared by magic!

"How did you do that, Pip?" I asked.

Pip just winked at me and smiled. What a very magical cat he is!

Butterfly proud said some days she only writes down one thing. Some days she writes down more things.

Then she started telling us about the list she has that helps her.

As she did, I started to write it down.

Butterfly Proud – My helpful list to choose from. I need to choose one or more of these things each day to add to my well-done jar

A kind thing someone has said to me

A kind thing I have said to someone

A kind thought I have had

Something someone has helped me with

Something I have helped someone with

Something I have done well – even when it was really hard and I wanted to give up!

Something I have learnt

Something I feel good about

Something I have given someone

Something someone has given me

When she had finished, Butterfly Proud said, "My **Well-Done Jar** makes me feel so good and proud of myself. Each time I add a note to my jar, it makes me want to sing. Just before you both arrived, Butterfly Anxious told me that my singing had calmed him a little bit. That made me feel good, so I was adding that to my jar as you arrived.

Some days when I feel a little bit sad or bored, I empty my jar and read all of the lovely things I have written. Then I feel much better about things again. I am very excited that you will be creating your own jars."

"Thank you so much, Butterfly Proud. I am very excited too!"

"Let's go back home." I said to Pip, "I am really excited about having my own **Well-Done Jar**."

Pip looked at me and said, "I'm really excited as well Mel. Yes, let's go home and get started!"

We said goodbye to Butterfly

Proud and went back home to start

our **Well-Done Jars**. How exciting!

Now we just need to decorate

them.

So lovely reader, when will you get started on your **Well-Done Jar**?

How will you decorate yours?

We do hope you have as much fun as we did!

MY WELL-DONE JAR

When I look at my Well-Done Jar,

I can see notes I have written so far,

It makes me feel really proud,

So much that I want to sing out loud,

People have done kind things for me,

And me to them, it's clear to see,

Kindness goes a very long way,

So, I put notes in my jar each day,

What have I written today so far?

Well, that deserves yet another star!

So, lovely reader, I'm telling you,

Start your jar and feel proud of you!

What helps Butterfly Believe

Be So Kind?

Hello again, lovely reader. Today is such a lovely day. I hope you are ready to go back to the butterfly farm.

Today I ask Pip if we can go back to see Butterfly Believe. When we met her last time, she was so busy helping the butterflies that she couldn't stop for long. I really want to find out how she helps the other butterflies. I want to learn how to do the same and to help you lovely readers too.

I don't know about you, but when I feel anxious, sad or angry, I find it harder to be kind to other people. I don't mean to, but sometimes I can be a bit unkind or have unkind thoughts. Then I feel bad for having them.

Butterfly Believe must be very kind because she looks after so many butterflies. She must be very clever too. I would like to be just like her!

So, are you just as curious as me to find out, my lovely reader? Let's go and see her and find out together!

As usual, Pip jumped up onto my bed. Once again, he pointed his tail at the snow globe. Once again, the orange light came out of the end of his tail and my snow globe lit up like magic. Then I heard him say:

'Tickety-Dee, Tickety-Boo,

What does Butterfly Believe really do?

Tickety-Boo, Tickety-Dee,

Let her show us – just wait and see.'

We arrived at the butterfly farm and it was lovely and sunny. Me and Pip could see so many butterflies flying around and enjoying the sunshine.

Then we saw a beautiful white butterfly flying towards us. There was only one white butterfly at the

butterfly farm, and I know her name is Butterfly Believe. I was so happy to see her again!

She landed on Pip's nose. Just as she had done before. Only this time, Pip didn't sneeze.

Butterfly Believe said, "Hello again Mel and Pip. How lovely to see you both! I do hope I get to spend some more time with you today. But you do know how busy I can be. If a butterfly needs me, I will need to leave."

"Of course." I said to Butterfly Believe.

I looked at Pip and said, "We understand, don't we Pip?"

"Yes, we do." replied Pip, "We have come back to the butterfly farm today to ask for your help, Butterfly Believe. Mel wants to learn how you are so caring and helpful to others.

Can you tell us what helps you to do this with such kindness?"

Butterfly Believe said, "I have learnt many skills over time, and I like to share them with the butterflies.

When the butterflies feel better about themselves, so do I. I also believe every butterfly and every one of your lovely readers can learn the skills I teach. Some may find them easy and some may need more help. All I ask is for them to try. As long as they try, that is all that matters.

I would like to show you something to learn about and practice. It is called **KIND-MIND**. It worked for Butterfly Anger the other day when she was getting her wings in a bit of a twist!

Would you both like me to show you?"

Pip and I both nodded and said, **'YES PLEASE!'**

Butterfly Believe started drawing something on a piece of paper.

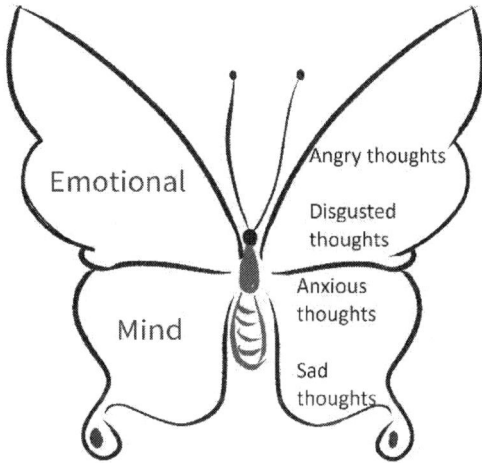

She had drawn a butterfly and wrote **EMOTIONAL-MIND** on the wings. She had also written different types of thoughts on the wings.

She said this was step 1.

She then asked if I had been feeling sad or anxious or angry or disgusted, or any other horrible emotions this week. I told her I had been feeling really anxious on Tuesday when I had been invited to Tom's birthday party.

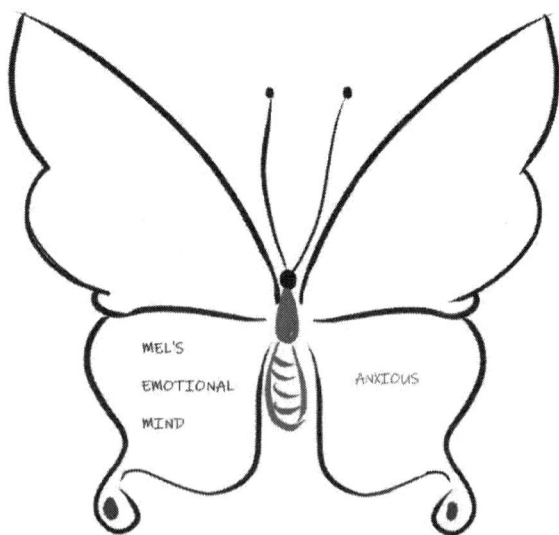

Butterfly Believe wrote down **Anxious** on **EMOTIONAL-MIND**.

Then she asked me what my anxious thoughts had been.

I told her all of my anxious thoughts. She wrote them down on **EMOTIONAL-MIND**.

Tom has a big dog called Max

Max barks a lot when I go and see Tom

I am scared of going to the party

MEL'S EMOTIONAL MIND

ANXIOUS

Tom has a big dog called Max

Max barks a lot when I go and see Tom

I am scared of going to the party

Butterfly Believe asked me what I wanted to do when I was thinking this way.

I thought about this. I told her I really wanted to go to the party because all of my friends would be there. But I wouldn't have to feel anxious if I stayed at home. So, staying at home was what I wanted to do.

She told me my anxious mind was stopping me from having fun.

Oh dear, that is so true! That isn't good at all, is it lovely reader?

Butterfly Believe smiled at me kindly. Then she started drawing something else on another piece of paper. When she finished, it looked like a picture of Pip's head.

It had **CURIOUS-MIND** written on it.

She said this was step 2.

Curious Mind

Then she said we needed to look at the situation like a curious cat. Just like Pip!

So, on another piece of paper, she drew the shape again. She then asked me some questions.

Does his dog bark?
Does he keep barking?

Do you enjoy going to Tom's house?

Then she wrote my answers down on **CURIOUS MIND**:

Tom says Max barks to say hello

Max only barks for a little while

I always have lots of fun at Tom's house

Tom says Max barks to say hello

Max only barks for a little while

I always have lots of fun at Tom's house

Butterfly Believe then asked me if thinking this way made me feel better about going to Tom's house.

I said, "Yes, but I am still feeling a little bit anxious."

Butterfly Believe said the final step would help me with my **'Yes, but.............'**

She told me that **'yes, but......'**

is what a lot of people do, which only

makes them feel even more anxious!

Then she put my **EMOTIONAL-MIND** and **CURIOUS-MIND** next to each other.

Tom has a big dog called Max

Max barks a lot when I go and see Tom

i am scared of going to the party

MEL'S EMOTIONAL MIND

ANXIOUS

Tom says Max barks to say hello

Max only barks for a little while

I always have lots of fun at Tom's house

On another piece of paper, she drew the shape of a heart.

She wrote **KIND-MIND** in the middle of it.

Kind Mind

She said this was step 3.

Then she looked at me and said, "Mel, we have your thoughts written down in **EMOTIONAL-MIND**

and **CURIOUS-MIND**. Now we need to mix them together a little bit. This will help us to work on **KIND-MIND.** This lets us to see things in a different way.

Because when we use **KIND-MIND,** we can learn to understand and accept that we have difficult emotions sometimes. This is really important because our emotions are very real. It is also okay to have them.

But we also need to be curious and think about things in a more sensible way.

I will do **KIND-MIND** in 3 steps, so that you can see for yourself.

We will call them **ABC**.

I will write some things down. All you need to do is fill in the blanks from what we have written already on the butterfly's wings and the cat's face.

It doesn't matter if you get stuck Mel. We will think about this together, and I will write them down for you.

Let's see what this looks like by starting with what we wrote on the

EMOTIONAL-MIND butterfly and add it to **A**."

A. It makes sense that I am feeling:

Anxious

Because:

I get scared when Max barks

Then she said, "Now let's now move onto what we wrote on the **CURIOUS-MIND** cat and add it to **B**."

B. But what I know is:

Max gets excited when people arrive. He just wants to say hello and he soon stops barking. I always have fun at Tom's house.

"Now let's do the final step and add it to **C.**" she said.

C. So, what I need to do is:

Remind myself that I don't need to feel scared of Max. He has never harmed anyone. He gets sent to his basket if he gets too excited. So, I am going to the party and I will have a fun time with all of my friends!

Kind Mind

A. It makes sense that I am feeling anxious, because I get scared when Max barks

B. But what I know is Max gets excited when people arrive. He just wants to say hello and he soon stops barking. I always have fun at Tom's house

C. So what I need to do is remind myself that I don't need to feel scared of Max. He has never harmed anyone. He gets sent to his basket if he gets too excited. So I am going to the party and I will have fun with all of my friends

So, my lovely reader, are you as excited as me to start practising and learning how to play the **KIND-MIND** game?

I found this game really helps to change my thinking. I am now really looking forward to the party without my anxious thoughts getting in the way!

But I know I will need to practice this game a few more times before it becomes easier for me. Do you think so too?

Perhaps we can practice it with some of the other butterflies as we meet up with them again?

Before we do this, let's say this poem out loud together!

Butterfly Believe is kind you see,

Believing in the best of you and me,

So don't stay in emotional-mind,

Because that can be so very unkind,

To you and me and everyone,

And we know that is not any fun!

So, first just notice how you feel,

Take a look at the butterfly wheel,

Then move over to curious-mind,

From there you will be able to find,

A sensible way to look at things,

Let's see what curious-mind brings,

Then on we go to our kind-mind,

This is the part that allows you to find,

A kind and helpful way to react,

A better way to think, feel and act,

I encourage you to play this game,

A happy kind-mind is the aim,

Be kind to others in whatever you do,

And remember to also be kind to you!

It is good to be curious and kind

Where Is Butterfly Sadness Hiding?

I don't know about you lovely reader,

but I woke up feeling really excited

about visiting the butterfly farm again

today.

This time I would like to see Butterfly Sadness. He was so very sad the last time we saw him. In fact, he was feeling so miserable and lonely, he believed that nobody liked him. No matter what we tried to tell him, he just wouldn't listen.

Now, I have just had a great idea lovely reader. If Butterfly Sadness won't listen to us, then we need to try something else.

What if we help him to work things out for himself? To find out that others really do like him? Then he wouldn't feel so sad and lonely all of

the time, would he? Let's help him with some of the games we have been learning.

Pip told me he thinks this is a brilliant idea! So, let's say Pip's magic rhyme together to create a little bit of magic, so that we can all help Butterfly Sadness together.

'Tickety-Dee, Tickety-Boo,

Let's teach Butterfly Sadness a game or two,

Tickety-Boo, Tickety-Dee,

Let's help him to see things more clearly.'

We arrived at the butterfly farm and it took us ages to find Butterfly Sadness. After a long time of looking for him, we found him. Poor thing, he was looking as sad as ever. I just wanted to make him feel better, so I started talking to him.

I said, "We've come back to see you, Butterfly Sadness. You are still looking so sad. How can we help you?"

Butterfly Sadness replied, "I don't think anyone can help me. I know I have seen you before, but I don't remember your name, little girl."

"My name is Mel and this is my cat called Pip." I said, "I sometimes feel sad too, Butterfly Sadness. When I do, I can feel things happening in my body. I can feel tired and tearful. Sometimes I don't even want to play

with my friends. Do you feel any of these things Butterfly Sadness?"

"Yes, I do Mel. I feel tired and fed up all of the time. I just want to hide away and cry. I don't want to feel like this, but I don't know what I can do to feel better."

"It really does feel horrible, doesn't it, Butterfly Sadness? Me and Pip have learnt some really good games to play. They have helped us to feel happy and proud, and to believe in ourselves. This is because we are learning to think about things in a more helpful way. Do you want

us to show you what we have learnt? We would love to be able to help you to feel better? Will you let us try and help you, Butterfly Sadness?"

Butterfly Sadness looked up at me and said, "I will try anything, Mel. Just show me what I need to do."

I was so pleased Butterfly Sadness wanted our help. Because even though it is okay to feel sad sometimes, we have learnt it is also good to take off those gloomy glasses! I remember wearing them in

our last adventures and they were no

fun at all!

Do you remember lovely

reader?

Well, I must say, I didn't look at all happy, did I?

So, I explained the **Well-Done Jar** Proud has hanging from her tree. How good it makes her feel every time she adds to it. How it makes her want to sing.

Butterfly Sadness seemed to like this idea. I noticed a tiny little smile on his face as I was telling him all about it. Me and Pip also showed him our **Well-Done Jars** that we had just finished decorating.

Butterfly Sadness told us he liked them very much. Then I showed him the list I had written in my book. The list that helped me and Pip when we started our jars. A list I hoped he could find helpful too.

Butterfly Proud – My helpful list to choose from. I need to choose one or more of these things each day to add to my well-done jar

A kind thing someone has said to me

A kind thing I have said to someone

A kind thought I have had

Something someone has helped me with

Something I have helped someone with

Something I have done well – even when it was really hard and I wanted to give up!

Something I have learnt

Something I feel good about

Something I have given someone

Something someone has given me

"Pip has a jar for you Butterfly Sadness. It looks just like Butterfly Proud's jar, but it is yours. Look, I have written your name on it. It is empty at the moment, so let's get started. Let's look at the list and see if there is anything you can add to it. Then you can hang it on your favourite tree."

Welldone
Sadness

"I don't think there will be anything to add, Mel," he said in a sad voice, "but I will give it a try."

I told Butterfly Sadness that trying would be a very good start!

Look, lovely reader, can you see that Butterfly Sadness has his gloomy glasses on? I think it would be

a good idea for him to put on a clear

pair, do you?

So, I asked Butterfly Sadness to

put on my clear glasses. I told him

they were magic glasses!

Then he sat on my lap and we

looked at the list together.

After some time, Butterfly Sadness said,

"Mel and Pip, I have found one! These glasses are wonderful! On the list 'something someone has helped me with'. You and Pip have helped me to start feeling better by teaching me new things! I can add this to my jar. Yippie!"

Well, that was one word I did not expect Butterfly Sadness to say! But it made me so happy I could burst! Me and Pip both clapped our hands.

Then Butterfly Sadness started to feel a bit sad again because he could not think of anything else.

We said he had done very well to find one, but he wanted one or two more. We told him that we would find one each for him if he wanted us to. He said he would like that very much. Then he smiled again.

"I found one," I said. "Something I have done well – even when it was really hard and I wanted to give up! - You spoke to us when we arrived, Butterfly Sadness. Even though you wanted to

be alone. You also tried hard to find something to put in your jar. You tried and you found one. Well done!"

"I have also found one for you Butterfly Sadness," said Pip. "Something I have helped someone with - You have helped us practice going through the list. Also, as we helped you, we can add that one to our jars too!"

"This has been so helpful Mel and Pip. Thank you so much," he said. "I feel so much better seeing paper being added to my jar. I can't wait to

decorate it tomorrow! It will give me something nice to look forward to."

We smiled at him and I said, "There is just one more thing we would like to show you before we go Butterfly Sadness. Butterfly Happy calls it his **1-2-3** game. He writes down positive things each day as he wakes up, and each night before he goes to sleep. He says it helps him to stay happy.

"So, come and sit beside me again and we can look at this together." I said, "It really is such a helpful game to play, Butterfly Sadness. Let's make a start."

So, we did. With Butterfly Sadness sitting on my lap.

Me and Pip helped Butterfly Sadness when he got a bit stuck.

This was what we wrote:

1 thing I like about myself:

My lovely blue wings

2 things I am good at:

Trying to help people

Flying

3 things I am grateful for:

This beautiful farm where I live

The flowers

People that help me

When we finished, Butterfly Sadness said this made him feel much better!

He said he would try his very best to practice it every day. He also said he would ask Butterfly Proud and Butterfly Happy for help if he needed it.

"That is so good to hear," I said. "I am very curious to see if these games work for you. I will come back one day and ask you."

"That would be lovely Mel," said Butterfly Sadness. "I will look forward to seeing you both again."

I do hope you enjoy practising these games, lovely reader.

Butterfly Sadness watches me,

Write 1 thing that I like about me,

Then he starts to do the same,

And joins me in this 1-2-3 game,

Now we write 2 things we're good at,

Writing on my lap, where he sat,

Next are 3 things we are grateful for,

*We've both found 2, we just need
1 more!*

He seems to be enjoying 1-2-3,

*I do hope he practises it daily, just
like me,*

Please, lovely reader, do the same,

*And feel good about you, by playing
this game.*

A Well-Done Jar is good to do,

For the butterflies, and me and you,

So, find a jar you can decorate,

An old jam jar works really great!

Paper, pens, and maybe a star,

You won't have to look very far,

Let's just see what this jar can bring,

Will it make you want to sing?

So do get started on your Jar,

Feel proud of who you really are!

How Can We Help

Butterfly Anxious?

I can't wait to visit the butterfly farm

again today. Are you ready to join

me and Pip again, lovely reader?

This time I would like to see Butterfly Anxious. He was so very anxious the last time we saw him. He even thought we were going to hurt him! Me and Pip would never do that. We just want to help him to manage his anxiety.

So lovely reader, shall we say Pip's magic rhyme together to create a little bit of magic for Butterfly Anxious?

It worked for Butterfly Sadness last time, didn't it?

'Tickety-Dee, Tickety-Boo,

What's the best thing for Butterfly Anxious to do?

Tickety-Boo, Tickety-Dee,

Help him to manage his daily worry.'

We arrived at the butterfly farm. I told Pip that I do love coming here. He said he does too.

As we were walking, we could hear some muttering coming from behind the tree.

Then we noticed it was Butterfly Anxious. He sounded like he was giving someone a telling-off! As we got nearer, we realised he was giving himself a telling-off! Poor thing, he sounded very annoyed with himself.

I slowly walked towards him because I know he gets very frightened.

Do you remember what happened before, lovely reader? When we caught him in the net? Do you remember how anxious he became? He thought we were going to harm him, but all we wanted to do was to talk to him. Me and Pip knew

we needed to be very gentle. So, I spoke to him in a very calm voice and said,

"We've come back to see you Butterfly Anxious. You are sounding very cross with yourself about something. How can me and Pip help you?"

Butterfly Anxious replied, "I am so cross with myself and it is making me feel really anxious. The more anxious I become, the crosser I get with myself. I really don't know what to do! I would really like it if you can

help me, because I don't like feeling like this Mel and Pip."

"Of course, Butterfly Anxious. We will help you as much as we can." I said softly, "when I feel anxious and worried, I can feel things happening in my body. I feel my tummy turning. My thoughts go round and round in my head. I breathe quickly, and I feel a bit shaky and tense. Then I just feel like crying, and I sometimes do! Do you feel any of these, Butterfly Anxious?"

"Oh yes, I do Mel!" he replied.

"I feel all of them. But I feel so much better knowing you get them too when you are anxious. I thought I was the only one!"

"That is good to hear." I said, "But they do feel horrible, don't they? Let's try and find a way to help you with this."

"That would be really good Mel." He said, "I am anxious about not being able to fly very well when I fly in a group. When I do, I don't fly very well at all! Every butterfly can fly so much better than me. I just don't

understand it. When I fly alone, or with Butterfly Calm, I really enjoy flying and I can fly really fast! I know I am good at it really!"

So, I told him all about the **KIND-MIND** game that Butterfly Believe showed us. He said he was keen to try it.

So, I drew the shape of a butterfly, just as Butterfly Believe did.

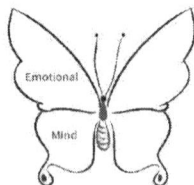

Then we started writing down

the worries he had told me about on

EMOTIONAL-MIND.

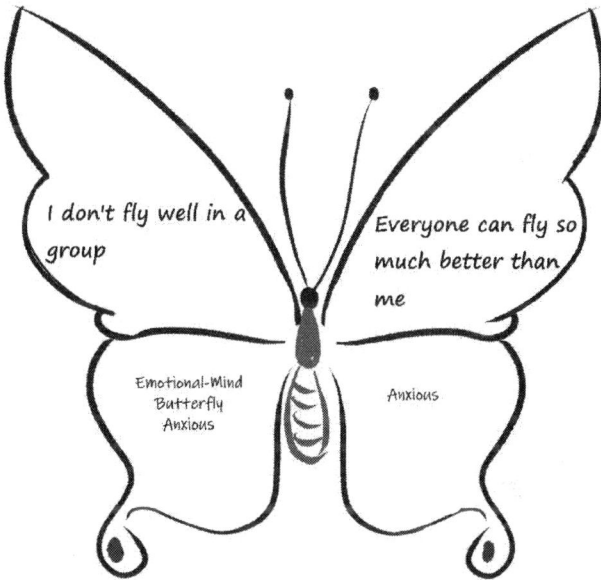

Then I said. "Let's help you let

go of those worries for a moment.

Remember, worries are just thoughts in our heads. Pip likes to let go of his worries by imagining the birds taking them away.

When he does this, he says he feels calmer and can think of better ways of thinking.

I like to blow my worries away. Just like Butterfly Calm. This helps me to feel calm and think in a more helpful way. Sometimes I have real bubbles and sometimes I imagine them in my mind.

As we were talking, we saw Butterfly Believe flying towards us. Then without stopping, she carried away all of Butterfly Anxious's worries with her. It was like magic!

Butterfly Anxious said he was
feeling much calmer because he
had let go of his worries.

We were now ready to work on
his **CURIOUS-MIND**. So, we wrote
down what he had said before.

When I fly alone or with Butterfly
Calm, I enjoy flying

I can fly a long way and really fast
when I relax

I am good at flying

He worked well with this, didn't
he, lovely reader? Now it's time to
look at **KIND-MIND.**

Do you remember how we do this, lovely reader? Let's go through the steps **ABC** again. Let's do this together because it will help Butterfly Anxious. It is also very good practice for all of us!

Here goes!

A. It makes sense that I am feeling:

Anxious

Because:

I keep thinking every butterfly can fly so much better than me

B. But what I know is:

When I relax, I can fly a long way, and really fast too! Even the bees can't catch me sometimes!

C. So, what I need to do is:

Remind myself that I am good at flying and that I can fly much better when I am relaxed. Then go and enjoy myself!

"I think this will really help me to fly and have fun with my friends," said Butterfly Anxious, "Thank you so much Mel and Pip."

A. It makes sense that I am feeling anxious, because I keep thinking everyone can fly so much better than me

B. But what I know is when I relax, I can fly a long way and really fast too! Even the bees can't catch me sometimes!

C. So what I need to do is remind myself that I am good at flying and that I can fly much better when I am relaxed. Then go and enjoy myself!

We told him we were very pleased to have been able to help him.

It was time for us to go. But then I had an idea! We had another helpful game to tell Butterfly Anxious about. Butterfly Calm's **Mindful** game of **5-4-3-2-1.** Do you remember it, lovely reader?

So, I told Butterfly Anxious all about it. That, as well as the balloon breathing of course!

5 is for five things I can see

4 is for four things I can touch or feel

3 is for three things I can hear

2 is for two things I can smell

1 is for one thing I can taste

I also told him that he doesn't have to feel anxious to play this game. That he can play it every day to help slow his worries down and calm his mind.

Then we thought of how we could practice it.

When he is flying, of course!

Perfect! He can focus on what is all around him when he is flying. That will take his mind off his worries!

So, when me and Pip both said '**ready**,' Butterfly Anxious took three long, slow deep breaths - in and out. Then he started to fly around us and said:

"**5** - I can see the tops of the trees. The clouds in the sky. The birds on the branches. The Bees buzzing around. The other butterflies flying here and there.

4 - I can feel my body relaxing as I fly. The lovely warm sun on my face. The gentle breeze through my wings. The softness of the flowers as I land on them.

3 - I can hear little children playing in their gardens. The birds tweeting. The sound of my wings flapping as I fly.

2 - I can smell lovely roses. The smell of freshly cut grass.

1 - I can taste the nectar from the cherry blossom tree.

Oh, I do love this game Mel and Pip, I'm going to play it every time I fly!"

It was so good to hear him say that. We wished him well and said goodbye. Then he flew off. I must say, he was flying very well indeed!

So lovely reader, is **KIND-MIND** making more sense to you now? I really do hope so. If not, keep practising like me and Pip do.

Also, how will you start letting your worries go? Will you use bubbles like me? Birds like Pip? Imagine

Butterfly Believe taking them away as she did for Butterfly Anxious? Or something else?

It is hard being anxious all the time,

So, listen to this helpful rhyme,

Emotions from the butterfly wheel,

Let us know how we really feel,

But don't stay on <u>STEP 1</u> for very long,

We do need to keep you moving along.

So do move onto your <u>STEP 2</u>,

Curious-Mind it is for you!

Just like Pip, my clever cat,

What do you really think about that?

Then on you go, to <u>STEP 3</u>,

Kind-Mind - the best place to be!

I know because I've tried it before,

It works for me, so I will do it some more!

I encourage you to play this game,

A happy Kind-Mind is the aim!

Just remember:

Be kind to others in whatever you do,

And remember to be as kind to you!

Kind Mind

Who Is Butterfly Disgust Talking To?

Another day to visit the butterfly farm.

I really do enjoy going there. I enjoy

helping some of the butterflies with

their difficult emotions. I also love to

learn and practice new games. Do you, lovely reader?

This time I would like to see Butterfly Disgust. The last time we saw her at the butterfly farm, she was really disgusted at something she saw. She was looking at a caterpillar breaking out of its cocoon and turning into a beautiful butterfly. But she was so disgusted, that she did not wait and see the beautiful butterfly hatch!

So lovely reader, let's say Pip's magic rhyme out loud to create a little bit of magic for Butterfly Disgust.

It worked for Butterfly Sadness and Butterfly Anxious, didn't it?

So, are you ready to join me and Pip again in our magical world at the butterfly farm?

Let's say it together!

'Tickety-Dee, Tickety-Boo,

What's best for Butterfly Disgust to do?

Tickety-Boo, Tickety-Dee,

Give her a lesson in curiosity.'

We are back at the butterfly farm. I am so excited to be here again! Pip looks excited too! Now, all we need to do is find Butterfly Disgust.

Then we heard her. She was near the pond. We could hear her voice and she was looking at something. She didn't look happy at all!

She was saying, "Ooh, that looks horrible! Ooh that smells disgusting! Yuk! Yuk! Yuk!"

"Hello" I said, "we've come back to see you, Butterfly Disgust. You are making a lot of noise. What is the

matter? Can me and Pip help you at

all?"

Butterfly Disgust replied, "This

pond is so disgusting. It looks and

smells disgusting! There are horrible

bugs that are so ugly! That area is brown and slimy. It makes me feel sick!"

I told her that we can all feel disgusted sometimes. Sometimes we feel disgust because it is something we don't understand. Something may look or sound or feel or smell or taste a bit strange. We may have seen someone else react this way. I also told her that I feel sick too when I feel disgusted about something.

In fact, the other day my baby cousin came to stay. Her name is Polly

and she is five months old. I do love Polly and she is very cute. But, when my aunt changed Polly's nappy, the smell was so bad that I had to put my hand over my nose! Polly had a snotty nose too!

At the time I had the same reaction as Butterfly Disgust. But then my aunt told me Polly had been unwell. That was why she had a snotty nose and a smelly nappy. That helped me to understand it better. Poor Polly has been unwell, so I gave her a big cuddle!

When I talked to Pip about this, he said that it can be helpful to be curious about things. Just like a curious cat. Just like he does. He said it would be good for me to practice taking a closer look at things. To ask

some questions about why things are

as they are. Not just react in disgust.

So, I told my story to Butterfly

Disgust and we agreed to try to

practice being curious together. Just

like Pip - my clever and wise curious

cat.

So, with the help of Pip, we started right away. Right there by the pond. We used the magnifying glass Pip gave to us.

I started first. I asked Butterfly Disgust if I could take a closer look at her and her beautiful green wings. She said she was happy for me to do that. So, I did.

Close up, she was amazing! I could see the scales on her wings. There were many shades of lovely green on them. Her eyes sparkled like green emeralds. Her body had lovely marks on it. She was really beautiful! I told her so and she smiled. She looked so pretty when she smiled.

Then it was her turn to practice. So, I asked Butterfly Disgust what she wanted to take a closer look at. Where she wanted to start to be like a curious cat.

She just winked at me and said, "Just wait and see, Mel."

Then she flew over to an area with lots of daisies. She had found a caterpillar. What a great idea!

She said, "Mel, I want to get a closer look at a caterpillar. I was once a caterpillar. One day it will turn into a beautiful butterfly. Just like I did!

Then she asked the caterpillar if she could take a closer look at it.

The caterpillar said her name was Cool. She also said she was

happy for Butterfly Disgust to take a closer look. So, I gave Butterfly Disgust the magnifying glass. Then she became really curious about Caterpillar Cool.

Then I heard her say.

"Caterpillar Cool, you have lovely shades of green all over your body. Just like me. You have a lovely

round face and kind eyes. Also, you have so many little legs! I really do like you. I hope to see you again when you have grown into a butterfly. I think you will be a very kind butterfly. Do come and find me and I will help you to make some new friends."

Caterpillar Cool then smiled the biggest smile. She was so very happy to have made a new butterfly friend. Even before she was one herself!

She looked so happy and so cute on her leaf!

Cool also started to become

curious about what kind of butterfly

she would turn into. What colour

would she be? What would her new

name be? Where would she live? Who would be her friend? This was a very exciting time for her!

But for now, she just needed to eat lots of leaves. She needed to grow big and strong to become the most beautiful and kind butterfly she wanted to be.

So, she said goodbye to her new friend Butterfly Disgust. She promised to find her when she was ready - when she had turned into a butterfly. Then she moved along the leaf until she could no longer be seen.

So, I asked Butterfly Disgust if being curious made a difference to her. How she felt about caterpillars and other things now.

"Oh yes!" she said. "Being curious like a cat is so much fun. I even made a friend. I do hope I see

Caterpillar Cool again. When she is a butterfly, of course."

So, lovely reader. Do you remember the last time you felt disgusted? Could being a curious cat help you too?

Well, it has really helped me. It has really helped Butterfly Disgust too. I do really hope it works for you too.

Let's read this poem to remind ourselves what we need to do.

Disgust is an emotion you may feel,

One emotion on the butterfly wheel,

So, when you start to feel disgust,

Like Pip, being curious is a must.

Look a little closer and you will see,

Curious cat is the way to be,

Seeing things with curious eyes,

May give you a very nice surprise.

Ask the questions you have today,

People will then hear you say:

When? Why? What? How?

Are you thinking differently now?

So, play this game and you will find,

You learn more with a curious mind.

Will Butterfly Anger

Ever Learn?

So, another day at the butterfly

farm. I can't wait to find Butterfly

Anger again. I remember her being so angry about everything! Not only were her wings red, but her face was really red too! In fact, she was red everywhere!

So lovely reader, let's go and find her. Let's say Pip's magic rhyme out loud to create a little bit of magic for Butterfly Anger.

It worked for Butterfly Sadness, Butterfly Anxious, and Butterfly Disgust, didn't it?

So, let's go and see if we can help her.

All together now – 1-2-3:

'Tickety-Dee, Tickety-Boo,

What's the best thing for Butterfly Anger to do?

Tickety-Boo, Tickety-Dee,

Help her to see a calmer way to be.'

We were back once more at the butterfly farm. This time we did not have to wait long at all to find Butterfly Anger. We could hear her

shouting! She was shouting very loudly! So, we followed the sound of her voice.

Once again, she was shouting at some young butterflies. She sounded very scary indeed! Those poor butterflies! They looked so very scared! We needed to help them as well as help Butterfly Anger. So, I asked Pip what we needed to do.

He said, "We need to speak to her in a calm voice Mel. We don't want to make her even more angry than she already is."

So, I took a few deep breaths.

Just like Butterfly Calm. Then I walked

up to Butterfly Anger.

I called up to her and said,

"Hello again, Butterfly Anger. Me and Pip have come back to see you. Can we please talk to you for a while? We know you are very busy, but can you stop to speak to us?"

"Well, the naughty butterflies have all flown away now!" She said, "I will speak to you for a little while, but I have to go back and find them again. They need to learn to do what I say!"

I thanked her and said that I was curious as to why she was so angry. Especially as Butterfly Believe

told us she had found the **KIND-MIND** game really helpful to manage her anger. I then asked if she was no longer finding it helpful.

She replied, "I can find all of my angry thoughts really easy! That is not a problem at all! But then I feel so angry that I can't think of any curious thoughts or any kind thoughts. I just get so stuck in **EMOTIONAL-MIND** with my angry thoughts! I was hoping **KIND-MIND** would be a helpful game for me. I really don't like being angry all of the time, Mel. It makes me feel

so tired and tense. Sometimes I feel angry at myself. Sometimes I feel angry at other people. Sometimes I just feel angry at everyone and everything!"

"Okay." I said, "let me and Pip help you try to get into **CURIOUS-MIND**. Would you like that?"

"I really would, she said. "I will try hard, but I'm not sure it will work."

So, she told us the angry thoughts she had. The ones she had before she started shouting at the butterflies this morning.

Butterfly Anger was right. She really did find this bit so easy!

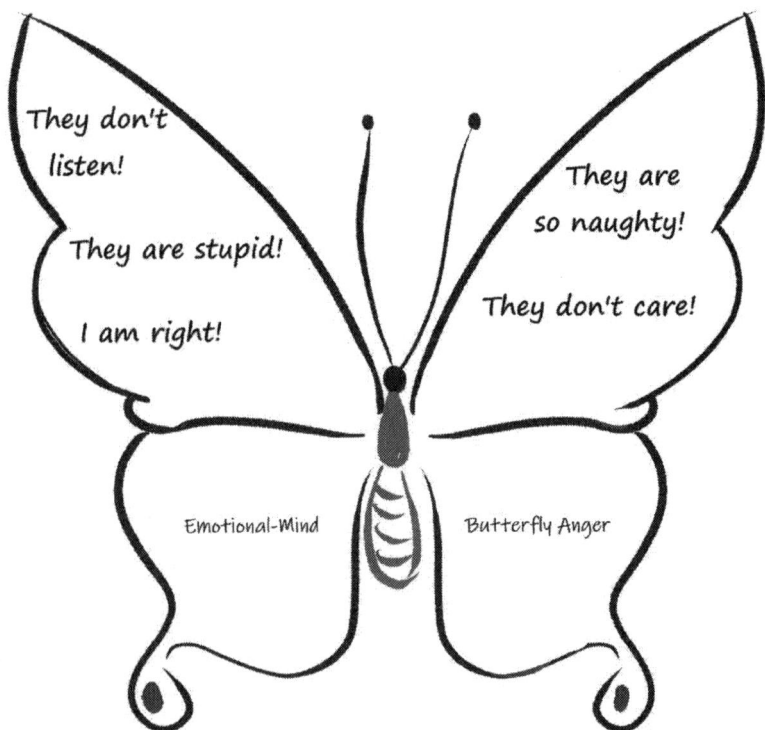

They don't listen!

They are stupid!

I am right!

They are so naughty!

They don't care!

Then Pip held up a **STOP** sign and said,

"We need you to be able to calm down a little bit so that you feel ready to work on your **CURIOUS-MIND,** Butterfly Anger. Mel has a good way to help herself calm down when she has angry thoughts. She blows bubbles and imagines blowing her angry thoughts away. This makes her feel calmer.

Then she is ready to use her **CURIOUS-MIND**. Just watch her for a moment."

And so, she did.

"Please may I have a go?" said Butterfly Anger. "I want to blow my angry thoughts away."

So, Pip handed her the bubbles, and she blew and she blew!

As she did, Mel and Pip noticed some pink areas forming on Butterfly Anger's red wings. Pink! Just like Butterfly Calm! It was working!

They clapped and told Butterfly Anger what they saw. She looked at her wings and said she liked the pink colour very much. Now she felt a lot calmer, she was ready to start working on her **CURIOUS-MIND**.

Then Pip said, "Ready when you are, Butterfly Anger."

Butterfly Anger replied, "Well I suppose they did try hard. They are

only little. They just want to have fun

and they did listen to me sometimes."

Then Mel wrote down what

Butterfly Anger said on **CURIOUS-**

MIND.

They did try hard

They are only little

They just want to have fun

They did listen to me
sometimes

"When you are ready, it is time to move on to **KIND-MIND** Butterfly Anger. Do you remember how to do this part?"

She said, "Yes, I do. I remember it's called **ABC**. I like this bit. Please write it down for me Mel."

So, Mel did.

A. It makes sense that I am feeling:

Angry

Because:

They don't listen to me sometimes

B. But what I know is:

They are young and playful and are
learning to fly well

C. So, what I need to do is:

Be more playful with them, so I can
enjoy teaching them to fly

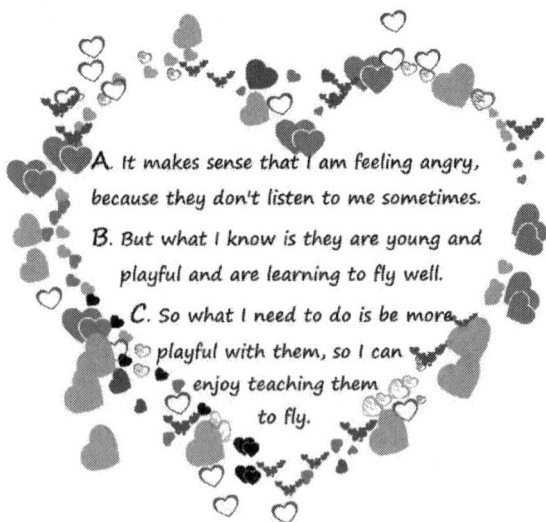

A. It makes sense that I am feeling angry,
because they don't listen to me sometimes.
B. But what I know is they are young and
playful and are learning to fly well.
C. So what I need to do is be more
playful with them, so I can
enjoy teaching them
to fly.

We asked Butterfly Anger if it had been helpful to play this game again.

She said, "It was much easier than the first time I played it because I remembered some parts. I also liked having a **STOP** sign so I could stop thinking about my angry thoughts over and over again. But what I really enjoyed was blowing bubbles! I could see parts of my red wings turning pink and I looked so pretty. I was feeling calm and pretty. That made me feel very happy."

I asked her if she would practice this game every day. She told me that she would.

She said she would imagine Pip holding up a **STOP** sign when she started to feel herself becoming angry. She would also imagine blowing bubbles before trying to work on **CURIOUS-MIND**. She would know when she was calm enough because she would be able to see parts of her wings turning pink, just like Butterfly Calm.

Butterfly Anger was now calm and it was time for me and Pip to go

home. So, we said goodbye and she flew off calmly to find the young butterflies.

I don't think they will be so scared of her now, do you lovely reader? I think she will enjoy teaching them if she can have fun with them too. What a lovely ending. That makes me feel really happy.

So, what have we learnt from this lovely reader? How can we best manage our anger? How do we know when we are feeling calmer?

Let's read the poem and see.

Feeling just like Butterfly Anger?

A STOP sign could be the answer,

Catch one angry thought at a time,

Write each down on a different line.

Then it is time for you to STOP!

Use those bubbles from the shop,

If you don't have any of your own,

Just imagine some you have blown.

Blow those bubbles and you will find,

You start to have a calmer mind,

When you start feeling less tense,

Thoughts will make a bit more sense.

With angry thoughts blown away,

Curious-Mind - it's time to play!

Then mix in with Emotional-Mind,

Now the final step is Kind-Mind,

A better way to think, feel and be,

Just like Butterfly Anger, Pip and me.

So, when you feel yourself feeling

anger,

These 3 things could be the answer:

STOP

Blow bubbles

Kind-Mind

Kind Mind

Bye For Now!

It is time for us to go again, lovely reader. We do hope you've enjoyed learning with us. We certainly have enjoyed being curious and learning about emotions from our beautiful butterfly friends.

Just for a bit of fun, we have added some activities for you to do at the end of this book. We do hope you like doing them as much as we do.

Love Mel & Pip x

Facebook:
www.facebook.com/melandpipbooks

www.melandpipbooks.co.uk

beverleydavies@melandpipbooks.co.uk

EXCERCISE 1: BALLOON BREATHING

Find somewhere you can relax. It may be on your bed, a sofa, a chair in the garden, or anywhere you want. When you are ready, practice your balloon breathing, just as Butterfly Calm does on **pages 11 & 12.**

EXCERCISE 2: WELL-DONE JAR

Do you remember Butterfly Proud's list

on **pages 52 & 53**?

Use it to help you think of things to

write in your very own **Well-Done** jar.

EXCERCISE 3: BLOWING BUBBLES

If you have some bubbles, just start to blow and imagine each bubble as a thought you want to blow away, just like Mel does on **pages 123 & 124**. If you don't have any real bubbles, then just pretend.

ABOUT BEVERLEY DAVIES

Beverley is a Cognitive Behavioural Therapist and a newly established children's author.

This second book in the Mel & Pip collection is a great addition to her first one, Mel & Pip & The Magic Snow Globe: Exploring Thoughts & Feelings.

Both are written as a fun and interesting way for children to learn about their thoughts, feelings, and behaviours, in the form of story-telling.

Beverley is aiming to enable children to better understand themselves and their experiences with interest and curiosity, whilst learning skills to manage difficult emotions through a variety of fun games.

Book 1 in the Mel & Pip series

AMAZON - ISBN: 9798796435687

Mel & Pip
&
The Magic Snow Globe:
Exploring Thoughts
and Feelings

Written by Beverley Davies

Printed in Great Britain
by Amazon